CHAPTER 1

PRESSING: AN ESSENTIAL TACTICAL ELEMENT IN THE DEFENSE PHASE

In this chapter we will be having a look at the meaning of the word 'pressing' and we will analyze the utility and the various different facets of one of the most widely applied collective strategies in modern soccer.

A DEFINITION OF PRESSING

Pressing is a collective tactical action, (i.e., carried out by more than one player), performed in situations of non-possession (also called the defense phase).

We should make a distinction between putting a player under 'pressure' and 'pressing' a player. Putting a player under pressure is an *individual action*, carried out in order to take away playing space and time from the opponent in possession. To apply pressing means that a number of players are cooperating simultaneously so as to reach a common aim.

It goes without saying that, in order to carry out good collective pressing, the individual player's ability to put an opponent under pressure can be necessary.

However, if we are to speak of *a team in pressing*, these are the prerequisites:

- our opponents are in possession;
- by following a pre-established strategy, a number of players are cooperating to regain possession.

WHY PRESSING IS USEFUL

The purpose of pressing is to close up the spaces and playing time for the team that is in possession, making it difficult for them to develop their attacking moves and easier for us to regain the ball.

TYPES OF PRESSING

One of the most widely used classifications to define the type of pressing put into action by a team is made in reference to the part of the field where these collective tactics are applied in the most systematic way. We often speak, therefore, of *ultra-offensive, offensive* or *defensive* pressing, depending where our active attempt to disturb the opponent's plays most frequently begins – in other words, from which of the lines identified in Fig. 1.

There are, however, other classifications that can be useful in describing how a team presses in the defense phase. We can distinguish between *sectorial* pressing; *whole field* pressing; *personal* from *general* pressing; pressing *forwards* from pressing *backwards*.

Sectorial pressing is different from whole field pressing because during the defense phase the team moves in to reduce the adversary's space and playing time principally when the opposing players are occupying certain parts of the field (i.e., if they are near the sidelines).

Personal pressing can be distinguished from general pressing because in the first case the team concentrates its collective plays principally when certain opposing players are in possession (usually those who present more difficulty from a technical point of view, or those who we consider to be more dangerous). In forward pressing the team carries out collective movements advancing into depth (as with ultra-offensive pressing, for example); in backward pressing, on the other hand, they are coming down field (as, for example, in defensive pressing with the mid fielders moving backwards and bringing themselves nearer to the backs in order to double up or to cover certain zones).

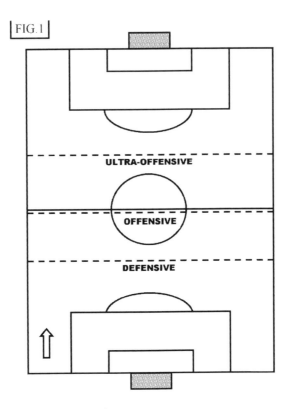

FIG. 1

ULTRA-OFFENSIVE

OFFENSIVE

DEFENSIVE

Apart from the type of pressing being put into use, the foundation on which we base the whole organization of this collective movement is what we call the *shift*.

In fact, the collective, collaborative movements identified as pressing are a development of shifting moves – defensive slides made towards the ball zone. In the next chapter we will be having a look at shifts.

Before entering into such an analysis, however, we must first consider the fact that the effectiveness of pressing can and often does depend on the part of the field where the player in possession happens to find himself. Without any doubt, it is easier to press your opponents when the ball is on the sidelines than when it is in the central zone. This is true because:

- Firstly, when the ball is near or around the sidelines, the player has natural limits to the direction in which

4

he can pass – towards the center or down the line. On the other hand, when the ball is in the central area, the opponent has 360° at his disposal in which to direct his plays.

- Secondly, as the ball approaches the sidelines, it divides the field in two, and we get a strong side (where the ball is being played) and a weak side (where it is not). At this point, the defending team can relax its marking on the weak side to allow for shifting moves towards the strong side, where it is more advantageous to create situations of numerical superiority or maximum individual pressure.

WHEN TO CARRY OUT PRESSING

Apart from the part of the field in which to apply it, there are other important factors to consider to make the most of pressing. The conditions that will give you the best results are when you go into pressing:

- on a player whose technical ability is not first rate;
- on a player who is about to receive a ball that it will be difficult for him to control (a high ball, a fast ball etc.);
- on a player who is about to receive in a difficult area (with little assistance from his team mates or in a position where he cannot afford to lose the ball).

Taking all these factors together, it will be clear that pressing can be carried out on the whole field – in a way that we could call 'surgical' – only in certain circumstances.

It is very important to find the right ways of teaching the players how to apply pressing so that they can understand and respond correctly to the directives given by the coach.

CHAPTER 2

SHIFTING

In this chapter we will be having a look at shifting. We will try first of all to understand what a shift is exactly, and then we will analyze its function, its purpose and the ways in which it can be carried out. These are the questions we will be trying to answer:

- what does shifting mean?
- why is it carried out?
- how can it be carried out?
- when should it be carried out?

A DEFINITION OF SHIFTING

A shift is a movement made by one or more players involved in the defense phase, who, following the team's strategies, its individual or collective tactical principles, move away from the original position on the playing field and go to take up another that is more useful from a tactical point of view. They do this in order to:

- regulate a concrete or a potential situation of numer ical inferiority;
- compress the opponents' playing space and time so as to create a situation of numerical superiority that will be to their own advantage.

To sum up: the word 'shift' originally identified the movement of one or two players, who, leaving the position they normally occupy in their playing system, converge on the area around the ball in order to close in on an adversary who has escaped the control of one of their team mates or who has been left free by the a defender who has himself had to make a shifting action. The concept of shifting has been modified somewhat by the introduction of total zonal marking. In the zonal defense system the defender has the ball, his team mates and the opponent as his points of reference; and he does not shift into the ball zone only to take the place of a team mate who has been passed by the adversary in possession. In a zonal system, the players shift into the ball zone in order to constrict the space and time that the opponent has at his disposition, and they do so whether or not the man marking the player in possession has let him through or not.

THE DIFFERENCE BETWEEN A SHIFT AND GETTING INTO AN ACTIVE POSITION

Both a shift and a movement to get into an active position are carried out so that the player can take up a new position where he will be tactically more useful than in his original one. But, while a shift has the purpose that we have already described and can be carried out by players placed both under and above the ball line, 'getting into an active position' is when the player finds himself above the ball line and in a passive position (i.e., in a position in which he will be able to do nothing to help the defense phase) – and so moves back in order to put himself in a position that will be of more use to his team's defensive aims.

PURPOSES: DEFENSIVE AND PRESSING-ORIENTED SHIFTS

Depending on the reason why the shift is done, we can distinguish between defensive shifts and pressing-oriented shifts.

Whereas *defensive shifts* are carried out for the tactical re-balancing of a critical situation (real or potential numerical inferiority), *pressing oriented shifts* aim to compress the adversaries' space and playing time during the course of a pressing action.

It is important to note that situations of numerical inferiority can come about as the result of the natural face off between two playing systems as well as because of our opponent's various plays and actions.

RESULTS

Both defensive and pressing-oriented shifts work best over short distances – when there is not a long stretch of field between a player's parting position and the place where he will be more useful tactically. Apart from this, the other fundamental considerations in order to maximize the shifting move are the *speed* with which the distance is covered and the way in which the player *reacts* to the situation. These two things – reactivity and running speed – are strictly related to the alertness and to the motivation of the player, apart, of course, from his physical and psychological form.

TYPES OF SHIFT

We can define a number of different ways of shifting in relation to the various different elements that are to be considered when speaking of the game of soccer.

In reference to the **various zones on the playing field** we can talk about *shifting on the weak* or on *the strong side*.

Shifting on the strong side is brought to bear on that part of the field that is near or around where the ball is in play, while shifting on the weak side comes about in the area of the playing field that is far away from the ball. The shifting moves on the weak side are usually a consequence of those carried out on the strong side. In cases like this the player of an advanced section moves backwards to integrate himself with the section below so that his team mates can move towards the area where the ball is in play.

In reference to the **starting position** (and, as a consequence, to the direction in which the player actually carrying out the shift is moving) we can classify the shifting movements themselves as *horizontal (or flat) shifts* and *vertical shifts*. Vertical shifts can then be subdivided into *forward* or *backward shifts*. When the player carrying out the shift begins his movement from behind the position he wants to reach, then we have a forward shift. If the position to be reached and the starting point of the shift are on more or less the same longitudinal line, then we have a flat or horizontal shift. When the player is trying to get to a point that is behind his original position, then we have a backward shift. Clearly, the shifting player will be in advantage – as far as timing and angle of vision are concerned – when he is moving forward (in particular when his aim is to confront an opposing player in possession). We should note that it is advisable to

10

carry out backward shifts only on the weak side of the field or in order to cover a player not in possession.

In reference to the direct adversary being in a **situation of possession or not** we can divide the shifts into: *shifts onto the player in possession*, *shifts to cover the player waiting for a pass* and *shifts on the player in support*.

In reference to the **number of players involved in the shifting movement**, we can distinguish *individual* from *collective shifts*.

Individual shifts are carried out by a single player whose movements are independent of his teammates'. A typical example is the shift made by the sweeper marking a single man to cover an opposing player in possession. With collective shifts, on the other hand, we are talking about movements made by more than one player at the same time. In cases like these, the movements of one player are strictly related to the movements of the others. While individual shifts are distinctive of teams playing man-marking, collective shifting is more characteristic of zonal defense tactics. Clearly, it is much more difficult to coordinate the timing of a number of players than to see a single man make a good individual shift.

In reference to the number of players involved, **collective shifts** can be subdivided into *section* or *chain shifts*. Players of a single section of the team are involved in section shifts, while in chain shifts the movement of a certain number of players forms a vertical chain. Section shifts can in turn be divided into horizontal or vertical shifts (when, for example, the section is in the form of the rhombus). Chain shifts, on the other hand, always move in a vertical sense, and the difficulties the team will have in carrying them out is in proportion to the number of players involved in them.

HOW TO SHIFT

In the last paragraph we had a fairly in-depth look at the various types of shifting moves. What we now wish to do is to pick out the most practical and the 'safest' shifts to make. We must always remember that *the ball can go faster than any player*, and so the team strategy must foresee shifting moves that are concretely – and not only theoretically – possible . The easiest shifts to carry out are those made when *the starting position of the player is further back than his finishing point*. It is important, therefore, that the team strategy calls for forward shifts into the 'ball zone'. Backward shifting moves are useful when you want to permit the team mates in your chain or in your section to converge on the ball zone, and they should be carried out *on the weak side or on adversaries who are not in possession*. In my opinion, the only useful type of backward shift on the strong side is when a player positioned 'forward' moves back to double up on one that is 'behind'.

DEFENSIVE SHIFTS

As we have already seen, defensive shifts are fundamental because they allow the team to compensate for a situation of numerical inferiority. We have also pointed out that such situations can derive from the opposition's attacking plays (i.e., a striker managing to dribble past our defense player) as well as being the result of the face off between the tactical playing system of the two teams. If, for example, we are using the 4-4-2 system and are facing a 3-4-1-2 – then the problem in the mid field will be how to shift in such a way as to contain the opposing attacking mid fielder.

In order to organize his strategy and to indicate the best defensive shifts, the coach must assess his own players' and the adversary's particular characteristics with some care. It is also a good idea to have a good look at the strikers' ability to defend, and to decide how and when their active position should be brought back and who should be involved in such moves. In the example that we have just mentioned – with the 4-4-2 facing a 3-4-1-2 – we could build up a defense strategy that will involve the backward movement of a striker in coverage on the opposing mid fielder not in possession (inside backward shift on the weak side). In this way, we have tactically readjusted the numerical situation in the central zone, and we are allowing two of our center players to align themselves vertically, one closing in on an opposing center mid fielder and the other moving back on the attacking mid fielder (Fig. 2). When our striker moves back he will clearly be creating a 3 against 1 situation in the adver-

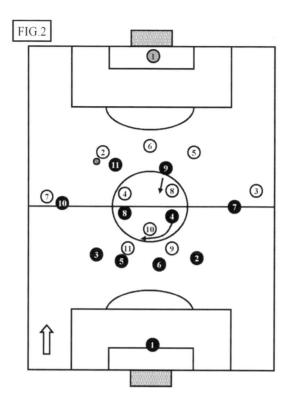

FIG.2

sary's favor along their line of defense, and, as a consequence, they will probably bring a defense player forward with the ball in order to create numerical superiority in the mid field. If this back goes towards the sideline, we will 'equalize' the situation with a forward shift on the part of our side chain (the mid fielder closes on the player in possession, with our side back moving up to cover the opposing side player). If the opponent's defender in possession comes forward through the central area, we will have to make a shift using the mid fielders, so 'freeing' the opposing attacking mid fielder and leaving him to be looked after by our defense section. In this second situation our four-man defense should be playing in a tight and compact way in order to exploit their numerical superiority (4 > 3) against the two opposing strikers backed up by the attacking mid fielder – and they will be able to do so because the side backs are not involved in shifts along the sidelines.

This example shows how the coach must make careful preparation for each match so that the team does not suffer in particular zones of the field as a result of the tactical situation created by the confrontation of the two systems. This book is not intended as a guide to identify the possible moves and countermoves for every tactical confrontation, (which have already been surveyed in 'Moves and Countermoves'). What we are now looking for are more universal keys to be used during the various matches. To readjust a situation of numerical inferiority, and wishing to do so by making a forward shift to close in on the opposing player in possession, we can carry out:

- a forward shift, compensated for by having the defense line cover a member of the opposition;
- a forward shift compensated for by a backward shift on the weak side.

The first case implies that the team section taking charge of the opposing player is able to cover an extra man *because they are in numerical superiority.*
The second case foresees that a player of a more advanced section will shift backwards – preferably *on the weak side* – in order to strengthen the part of the team left in numerical inferiority.
We had a look at both these cases when taking the example of the 4-4-2 against the 3-4-1-2. As we saw, in fact, the forward movement of the opposing back was covered by a shifting movement that left an adversary to be looked after by the defense line. If the back is moving forward along the sidelines, the opposing side mid fielder is left to our nearest side defender, with our side mid fielder shifting forward in coverage on the player in possession (Fig. 3).

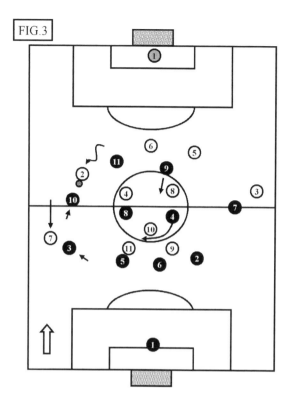

FIG. 3

In cases where the defense player in possession is advancing in the central area, our forward shift will be carried out by our center mid fielders, and their attacking mid fielder will be covered by our defense line. (Fig. 4)

As well as this, as we can see in the example, the situation of numerical inferiority in the mid field can also be made up for by the backward movement (shift on the weak side) of a striker and the downward shift of a mid fielder closing in on the rival attacking mid fielder. It goes without saying that these are only a few of the various possible solutions. In themselves even these would probably need more in-depth analysis and development, and there are other movements that could be used with the same force and validity. Another problem that the coach must look into and resolve when he is planning how to counteract the opposition's system of play comes out of his *study of placement*. An example will make this con-

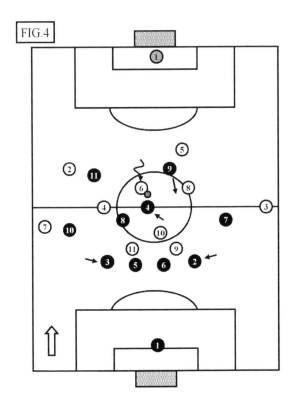

FIG.4

cept easier to grasp. If I am using the 3-5-2 and I find myself facing a team drawn up with the same tactical system, then the summit of both teams' mid field section will be lying low and we will have difficulty closing in on our man. In this sort of case, even though there is numerical equality we must decide on the best shifting moves so that the player who is in a 'favorable position' cannot act with too much freedom. Here we want to close in on a player who is operating in the central area, and either one of the center mid fielders can shift forward as seen in the two following examples (Fig. 5 and 6) or we can shift backwards bringing down a striker (Fig. 7). These solutions foresee that the team can move in the following ways:

- forward section or chain shift;
- allowing the direct opponent to advance;
- a team mate from a more advanced section can move backwards in coverage.

FIG.5

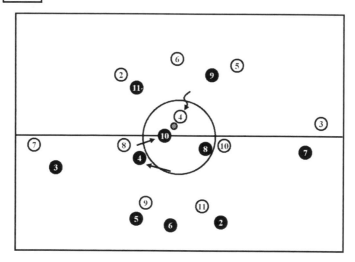

FIG.6

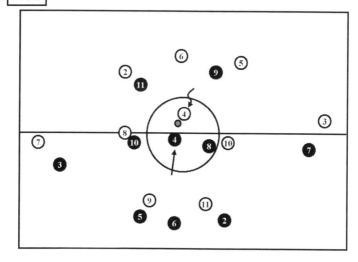

17

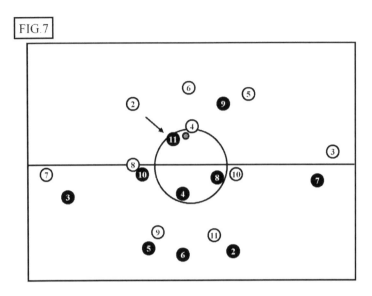

FIG.7

PRESSING-ORIENTED SHIFTS

The difference between defensive and pressing-oriented shifts is that the second are carried out in order to *create difficulties for the opposition's plays*. If we want to play in an aggressive way, our team must be well placed on the field and each member must be able to follow the common directives with verve and with the right timing.
As we have already said, and as indicated by the expression itself, pressing-oriented shifts will help the team develop good all round pressing whether you are applying it in defense or in attack.
An example of pressing-oriented shifts is when the side mid fielder moves back to double up on the opposing player in possession who is already covered by our side back (Fig. 8).

Another example of pressing-oriented shifting moves is shown in Fig. 9. The various players are slipping into the ball zone and they are ready to attack the adversary in possession by putting individual pressure on him or by closing up the lines into which he could pass the ball to his nearby support.

18

FIG.8

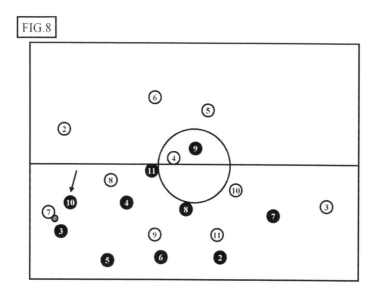

FIG.9

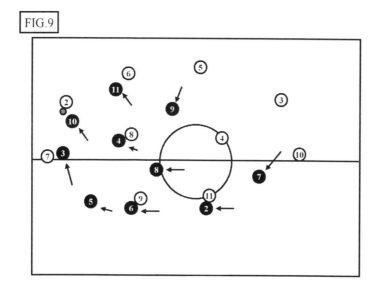

19

THE DIFFERENCE BETWEEN PRESSING IN DEFENSE AND IN THE ATTACKING ZONE

We have already seen that the use of pressing means putting your opponents under pressure in order to make it difficult for them to develop their attacking plays. In other words, we can identify pressing as the attempt to create a situation of numerical superiority in the ball zone by the best use of a technique known as shifting. On this basis, we must underline the fact that pressing is an element of collective tactics that can be brought to bear by teams that are using man to man marking as well as those playing with a zonal defense system. In other words, you do not have to be applying a zonal defense system in order to carry out effective pressing – though, of course, it will help the timing of your shifts if you are.

In my opinion, good pressing carried out in defense is something very different from that used in attack. The opposing player in possession will behave in a very different way depending on whether he finds himself attacked in his own half or in his opposition's. A side back, for example, who is being attacked in his own half will make an attempt to get rid of the ball without losing it rather than risk a difficult pass or try to defend it on his own. In the offensive half of the field on the other hand, because the team that is attacking has better chances of recovering the situation if they lose possession, the same side back will feel readier to pass the ball or try to get through himself. Even as regards getting rid of the ball, the side back in his own half will probably go for the long pass, while in the adversary's half his long pass will look more like a cross (which is more dangerous than a long pass pure and simple). The essential differences between pressing in the attacking and the defense zones are the following: a team that is defending with low level pressing will have to put a lot of pressure on the ball as well as either covering or doubling up, and on any supporting players (tight marking); apart from covering open spaces in order to regain loose balls. Instead, teams that are using ultra-offensive pressing must be good at putting the opponent in possession or his nearby supporting players under individual pressure. Another vital thing will be the team's ability to keep itself compact (creating favorable situations of numerical superiority) in the zone where long passes are arriving in order double up on an opponent who has gained possession or to capture loose balls. Another difference between the two is the way in which the team handles critical situations. Teams pressing in the attacking zone very often make use of tactical fouls of play to resolve difficult situations, while teams that are using low level pressing will normally put a player in coverage when they want to re balance a tactically difficult situation. The fact is that teams which try to attack opponents in possession when they are still in their own half have to accept situations of numerical equality in their defense section; besides which, they will be in trouble when their opponents send the ball into depth, because, at that point they have to manage a large part of the field behind the defense line. In such contexts, it is vital to crush at once any forward movement by a player with the ball at his feet who is trying to filter it towards the strikers. On the other hand, teams which are pressing only in their own half are more careful to control the opposing strikers (these being the players nearest to the goal to be defended); their defense section is often in numerical superiority and is able to make effective shifting moves and absorb the rival mid fielders as they break into the lines.

As well as that, strategic preparation for pressing in the defense and the attacking zone are different things. With teams that carry out low level pressing, what you need to perfect are positive density of players around the ball area, doubling up and covering; while the keys to in-depth pressing are closing off the points of reference and covering the lines into which the ball can be passed.

Before we begin to look at the two different ways of counteracting the opponents' plays, we must first try to identify the universal guide lines that the coach must build up, independently of the type of pressing he wishes to apply.

In laying down his strategic plan for the defense the coach must:

- establish whether, once they have lost ball possession, the team should immediately attack the opponents trying to regain the ball or move back and regather;
- decide the part of the playing field where the team is

to start going into pressing (both when the opponents are putting the ball back into play and when
the have gained possession as the outcome of a nor-
mal defensive move);

- decide which defensive technique to use most frequently in order to regain ball possession (doubling
up, anticipation, covering, etc.);
- define in which parts of the field to force the opponent's plays most frequently;
- establish guide lines concerning alternatives to the
basic team strategy;
- identify what possible solutions will best resolve critical situations.

CHAPTER 3

PRESSING IN THE DEFENSE ZONE

PRESSING IN THE DEFENSE ZONE

We have just seen that applying pressing in the defense zone means waiting for the opponents to arrive up to a certain part of the field before beginning to put the prepared strategy into real effect. Defense pressing is usually based more on covering the spaces rather than on aggressive play, on the ability to tighten marking at the right moment rather than making risky shifting moves. Teams that use this type of defense strategy normally have numerical superiority in the defense line over the opposing strikers. Following on from this, the most important techniques for carrying our effective defense pressing are these:

- individual marking (both on the player in possession and on his teammates in support);
- contrasting;
- doubling up;
- covering.

MARKING

Marking is the control of an attacking player carried out by a defender.

As tactics have evolved with time, so has marking undergone various transformations.

In modern soccer almost all teams use a (more or less evident) defensive zone, and so the defender is no longer the man controlling an adversary that has entered in his area of competence; now he must position himself so as to be useful even in cases when a nearby team mate covering a player in possession had let his man get by. In other words, a modern defender must be able to mark as well as cover.

We will now have a look at the aims of a defender when he is marking.

He must place himself so that *he can see both the ball and his direct opponent, making sure that the striker cannot receive the ball in depth.* This is a defender's first essential target. Another important objective is to

24

place himself in such a position that *he can attempt to anticipate* and regain ball possession in cases when the ball has been passed to his direct adversary.

If the adversary manages to receive the pass, then the defender must use the most appropriate defense technique in order to get back ball possession.

We will be having a look at these techniques at a later date, when we are talking about the work and the aims of the player going in contrast on an opponent in possession.

Let us now make a classification of the ways in which marking can be carried out:

- 'T' marking;
- marking in the cone;
- marking in anticipation.

In 'T' marking the control is fairly elastic.

This type of marking is carried out *on the weak side*, i.e., on a player far away from his team mate in possession. The T is a useful way of subdividing the part of the playing field that separates the defender from the striker so as to make a theoretical distinction between the area nearest to the defender and that nearest to the striker. The long arm of the T represents the half way point between the two and marks out the possible points where the defender can close in on the striker who has received the ball. Theoretically speaking the 'T' can help us understand in what part of the field the striker might receive the ball and where the defender will be able to contrast him. It is, of course, essential that the defender should be able to close in on the striker before he can shoot from a favorable position.

We must make a couple of considerations in order to define what we mean by 'a favorable position'. With the aid of computers we are now enabled to compile and study exact statistics concerning the shooting phase in general and the precise positions on the field from which winning shots are carried out in particular. The study of these statistics, both as an overall picture and as far as each single player is concerned, will allow us to mark out the particularly dangerous zones where it is especially important to close off the striker. In the near future, coaches of professional teams will probably be able to use computers in a decisive way. They will insert data about a single individual relative to each goal scored or even for each shot made, and they will be able to see the exact place from which the shot was carried out, even in cases when it was not actually successful. Looking at this in connection with other information, they will be able at once to decide which is the dangerous zone as far as each single player is concerned, as well as for the whole team their own side is to meet. In Fig. 10 and 11 we can see the T marking for two players covering their direct opponent. In the first case (Fig. 10) the marking is right because the closing line is outside the dangerous zone, while in the second case (Fig. 11) the marker is not placed correctly because this striker's ability in shooting from far off has widened the dangerous zone with the result that the closing line is no longer outside that area.

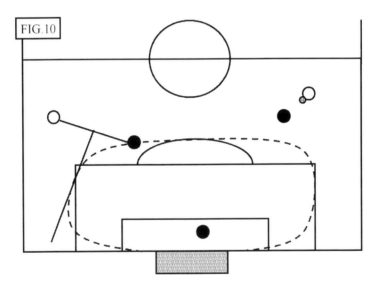

FIG. 10

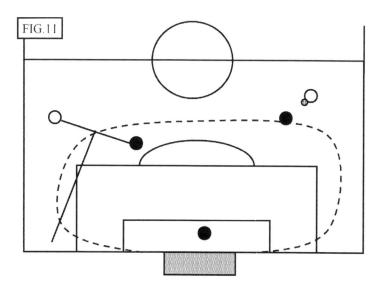

Having seen T marking, we can go on to take a look at *marking in the cone*.

This type of marking refers to the position taken up by a defender who is placed inside an imaginary triangle (or cone) which has as its base the goal line and as its summit the striker who is to be controlled. This position allows the defender to stand between the striker and the goal he is defending so that the striker cannot receive a ball in depth, but the defender can try to anticipate the ball if it is passed to his direct opponent. In any case, this placement will allow the back to block the striker's way even if he has received the ball (Fig. 12).

In relation to the striker's characteristics of play, it is important that the defender is aware of how close to his direct opponent he should place himself. Close marking makes it easier for the defender to anticipate, but it also allows the striker to attack him in depth. 'Blander' marking makes it easier to control the striker's in depth acceleration, but it reduces the chances of anticipation. T marking is usually carried out on strikers that are far from the ball; the defender will want to place himself inside the cone when the opponent is near the ball. In such cases it is in the defender's interest not to con-

27

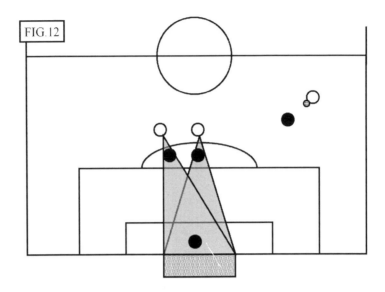

FIG.12

cede depth to the striker while at the same time giving himself the chance to anticipate if he can, or put extra pressure on his man should he gain possession.

Let us continue our survey of marking by turning to the question of how to place yourself in order to anticipate. Being able to anticipate your opponent before the player in possession has even carried out the pass, calls for a carefully defined defensive strategy. In fact, for each player placed in a way that allows him to anticipate, there must, in fact, be another connected team mate whose job it is to cover him and enter into action whenever the defensive play has failed and the anticipating player's direct adversary has gained possession and is ready to develop the attacking action.

In Fig. 13 we can see an example of how to place yourself in order to anticipate with relative precautionary coverage.

It is also a good idea to position yourself for anticipation when the player in possession is under so much pressure that he cannot play at his ease (situation of *ball coverage*).

We will conclude our reflections on marking by having a look at the control of the direct opponent inside the area. We have already seen that one of the principle aims of the defender is to place himself in

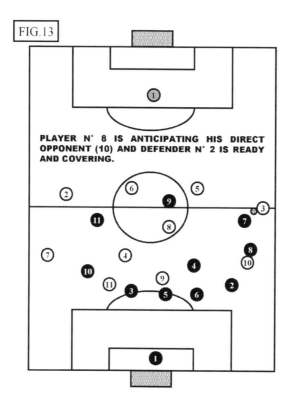

FIG.13

PLAYER N° 8 IS ANTICIPATING HIS DIRECT OPPONENT (10) AND DEFENDER N° 2 IS READY AND COVERING.

such a way as to be able to see both the opponent to be marked and the ball. However, it is not always possible for the defender to get into the best position. Very often the striker will make an attempt to escape from the defender on his blind side (moving away from the ball) with the very intention of making it as difficult as possible for him to control both the player and the ball at one and the same time. If you cannot both see the ball and at the same time as manage to control (even with physical contact) your direct adversary inside the area, it is important that you should concentrate on the man. Marking strikers in the area means that the defender should be trying to anticipate because whenever the striker arrives first to the ball he will in the dangerous position of being able to shoot at goal. If the defender just cannot anticipate he must in any case use what we call 'dirty' marking to stop the striker from taking up the best position or from jumping higher to head the ball. 'Dirty' marking is one of the principal aims of a defender controlling a striker near the goal. It requires the use of physical contact without having the referee give a foul against you.

CONTRASTING

When a defender faces an adversary in possession this is called 'contrasting the ball'.
A defender may have to contrast a player placed:

- in front of him;
- at his back;
- at his side.

We must also note that the player doing the contrasting can:

- bide his time without putting too much pressure on the player in possession;
- concentrate on making sure that his man does not carry our certain plays (forward passes, dribbling, etc.);
- try to regain possession (maximum pressure).

It goes without saying that by biding his time the defender is trying to slow down the forward development of his opponent's play – allowing the adversary in possession to conduct the ball while he waits for a more favorable tactical situation to evolve on the field. We have medium level pressure on the player in possession when we are trying to make sure that he cannot carry out particular plays that could create difficulties for the defense section (passes into open spaces, bringing the ball forward, crossing, dribbling).
Maximum pressure is when the defender – protected by his team mates and in a position, therefore, to risk the possible failure of his play – tries to intercept and regain possession.

CONTRASTING THE BALL

Let us now have a more specific look at what we mean by contrasting the ball, attempting to list the important things a defender must carry out in order to conclude his play in the best possible way.

The defender must everything possible to make sure that his rival cannot get past him. It is better to give space to your opponent rather that let him get around you. This first rule is always true except when your adversary is so near the goal that he could try a dangerous shot without considering the defender's choice of tactics. If it is important not to let yourself be dribbled, it is equally important, however, not to give your adversary all the space he wants as he is advancing.

The defender must bring himself near to the possessor as quickly as he can. The best thing of all is if the defender can already get into position during the 'passing time', in the brief moment before the striker manages to receive and control the ball. It is easier to intercept the ball, in fact, immediately after the striker has received it, when the stopping and controlling it make it more difficult for him to defend it.

The defender must be very careful to decelerate before arriving in close contact with the striker so that he does not arrive off-balanced, which might result in him being jumped at once.

The defender usually has his back to the goal as he is facing his opponent; the strikers on the other hand are facing the goal either when they are centrally placed or to one side or the other.

Having underlined the importance for the defender not to let himself be jumped and of crossing the space that separates him from the player in possession as quickly as possible, let us now look at how to contrast an adversary facing the goal who is making an attempt to get past.

When the defender has entered the zone of contrast (i.e., the tract of field from which he can intervene on the ball) he must 'accompany' the striker for a moment or two so as to 'tune in' on his forward speed. It is very important for the defender to follow the striker's movements briefly; at the same time, however, he must take the initiative.

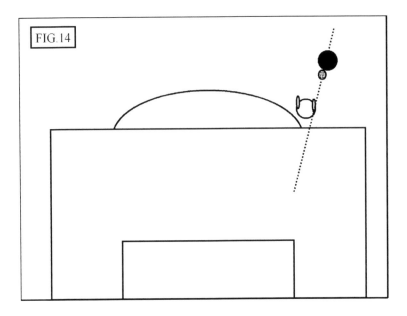

The position that the defender must take up in relation to the striker in possession requires that the contrasting player should not be too rigidly upright, but on the contrary that his legs should be slightly flexed making him ready to move in any direction, and that he should be placed at an oblique angle so that his right foot should be behind if he wants to force the striker to move towards the right or his left foot behind if he wants his adversary to move towards the left. The foot that is behind should be in a line with the ball as it is advancing as we can see in Fig. 14.

Taking the initiative can mean forcing your opponent to move towards a certain part of the field where we know we can be helped by a team mate. It can also mean – in cases where it seems a good idea to try and intercept the ball – making a dummy contrast, first of all, in order to modify the striker's attitude, which will no longer be that of making directly for the defender but that of trying to defend the ball, and then attempting to carry out a concrete intervention in order to regain possession or to obstruct the opponent's forward movement.

Just as it is important not to be jumped, the defender must limit interventions where he slips to the ground to those single cases where he is sure that he will get the ball or when such a move is a last ditch attempt to resolve a critical situation.

If the player in possession has his back to the goal it is very important for the defender not to go too near the striker or force himself into a move that might result in a foul. The defender must intervene when his opponent will be least able to protect the ball – that is, the moment when he is trying to turn with the ball. It is important, above all with players who are physically strong, to be careful that they do not use you as a sort of hinge. When they have their backs to the goal, many strikers like to feel the defender at their shoulders so that they can, with the help of their arms or their trunk, wheel around him and shoot.

The following is a summery of the important points that the defender should keep carefully in mind:

- avoid forcing your intervention, avoid committing a foul and make sure your rival does not get past you;
- close in on the striker as quickly as you can;
- take up your position with respect to the line in which the ball is coming forwards;
- follow the striker's movement for a moment of two;
- take the initiative;
- intervene only the moment when the striker is not covering the ball very well;
- avoid falling on the ground, unless it becomes indispensable.

Depending on the position of the player in possession, we can point out that the defender with his rival in front of him should bide his time when the tactical position is not favorable. When he is being covered by a team mate, he can attack the player in possession with greater intensity (limiting the range of his possible plays and letting him carry out only the ones that seem less dangerous). He can make an attempt to attack the ball only when he is sure that this will be successful or when the possible failure of his action will not be too great a risk. When the opponent is behind the defender it is much more difficult to force an intervention without committing a foul. In cases like these, the defender's principle aims are to make sure the striker cannot turn round and filter in a pass or dump the ball.

INVITED CONTRASTS

Invited contrasts are a fundamental technique in good pressing. We have an invited contrast when a player without the ball moves out on an opponent in possession with the aim of 'forcing' him to carry out a particular play. An invited contrast is carried out, for example, by a striker who decides to go in and force an opposing defender's play or that of a back who is biding his time waiting for a team mate to double up. We will now have a look at the tactical rules regulating the striker (or mid fielder) who is carrying out a good invited contrast.

You must not come out to contrast a defender when your own team mates are badly placed or in the distance. The only case in which it is right for a striker to put individual pressure on the back is when he feels that his opponent might find it difficult to control the ball, or when by bringing immediate pressure to bear he might be able to induce him to make a long pass. On the contrary, when his team mates are near at hand it is a good idea to come out against the opposing defender in possession for a number of reasons:

- in any case, even if the defender's pass to a mid-fielder in depth has gone past him, the striker can still and <u>as quickly as possible</u> go and take up a useful active or passive position of reference;
- when his team mates are in their right places it will be <u>much easier</u> for them to press and take space away from their opponents.

To sum up, it is wiser to wait a moment before coming out against the defender in possession even if that will enable him to move forward. It will also give the team time to get compact, while if you come out too quickly the team will be too long and loose.

In conclusion, it is best to attack the defender as shown in Fig. 15, coming up to him on the opposite side from the one in which we want him to play the ball.

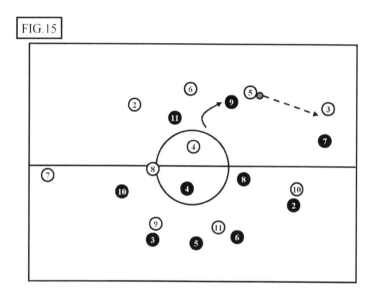

If we are carrying out our invited contrast in order to await the arrival of a team mate who is moving back to double up, then the defender must be able force the striker with the ball to slow down his forward movement, and at the same time he must be able to induce his man in a direction that will be the least favorable to the development of his attacking play or in such a way as to make things easier for the team mate who is coming back to double up.

DOUBLING UP

Having now made a close analysis of individual contrasts let us now have a look at the technique of doubling up. As the expression itself will tell you, doubling up is an intervention made to help a team mate near to a defender already occupied in contrasting a player in possession. As some experts point out, doubling up is not a movement made by two players moving in at the same time to attack an adversary in possession; it is created, rather, by the movement of one player, who, as he goes in to contrast an opponent in possession who is already under pressure and being controlled by a team mate, so creates a two against one situation.

Other people define the doubling up of marking as a tactical task carried out in the defense phase by two team mates aiming to take away space and playing time from an opponent with the ball and to regain possession.

WAYS TO CARRY OUT DOUBLING UP.

You can double up in various parts of the field, though it goes without saying that the defenders' work will be that much easier when the player in possession is situated near the sidelines. In such cases, of course, the adversary will not be able to pass the ball in certain directions, and the defenders will find it easier stop him moving forward or towards the center.

We are here talking about two players working together, and so the specific task to be carried out by each individual must be clear to both if they are to obtain a favorable outcome and if their doubling up is to be well structured from a tactical point of view.

The minimum aim of doubling up is to make it difficult for the opponent in possession to move forwards. Speaking generally therefore, it is important that the defender who is marking should take up position in the defensive cone, and that his team mate who is moving in to double up should place himself on the inside zone of the field.

The principle aim of doubling up, however, is *to regain possession of the ball*. Considering things in this light, it is important to say that one of the two defenders should be trying to stop the opponent's forward movement towards the goal, while the other should be concentrating on the ball in order to get it back. The player who is trying to regain possession should be the one who finds himself in the better position to succeed in doing so successfully.

At this point it becomes important to consider *direction* in which the player actually doubling up is running in, and the *position* and *orientation* of the player in possession. You can double up by moving forwards, and this happens when the player doing so is moving into depth (Fig. 16).

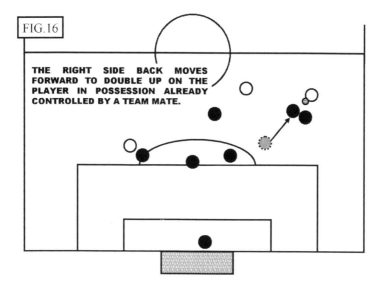

FIG.16

THE RIGHT SIDE BACK MOVES FORWARD TO DOUBLE UP ON THE PLAYER IN POSSESSION ALREADY CONTROLLED BY A TEAM MATE.

However, doubling up is normally carried out by a *down field* movement, when a player, finding himself too far up with respect to the position of the ball, tries to return into an active position by moving backwards and doubling up on the ball (Fig 17).

When he is doubling up, it is very important that the player moving in to help has a clear idea of what his task requires, the aims that are involved and the ideal position for him to take up in reference to his team mate.

The player going in to double up must help his team mate to regain possession. Generally speaking, he can do so by carrying out one of these two actions:

- he can intervene on the player in possession in order to regain the ball himself;
- he can place himself in such a way as to favor his team mate's intervention to regain the ball.

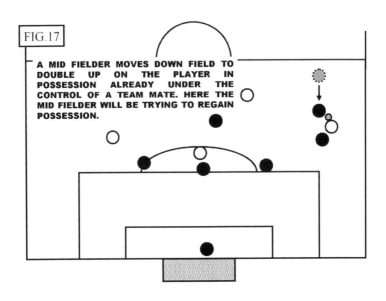

FIG.17

A MID FIELDER MOVES DOWN FIELD TO DOUBLE UP ON THE PLAYER IN POSSESSION ALREADY UNDER THE CONTROL OF A TEAM MATE. HERE THE MID FIELDER WILL BE TRYING TO REGAIN POSSESSION.

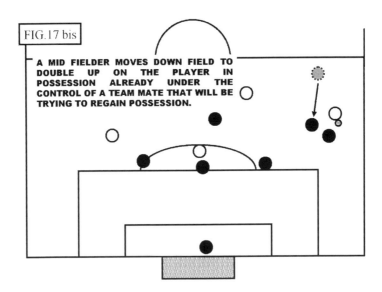

FIG.17 bis

A MID FIELDER MOVES DOWN FIELD TO DOUBLE UP ON THE PLAYER IN POSSESSION ALREADY UNDER THE CONTROL OF A TEAM MATE THAT WILL BE TRYING TO REGAIN POSSESSION.

The position of the player in possession will be the deciding factor, determining which of these two options is the better to apply from a tactical point of view. When this opponent is facing the goal as in Fig 17b the player moving back to double up should place himself to one side of his adversary so as to make sure that he will not move towards the center. This will favor the intervention of the direct defender.

Instead, when the player in possession has his back to the goal (Fig. 17) it will be easier for the mid fielder carrying out the doubling up to attempt to win back the ball, with his team mate taking up the best position to make sure that their opponent cannot turn and get away from them towards the center.

COVERING

Tactically speaking, covering is a very important task. You can cover an opponent in possession or one without the ball. Covering can be carried out by a defender who is marking his adversary at the same time, or by a defender who is not marking.
Covering the player in possession serves a double purpose. A defender in coverage can, as necessary, regain possession from a forward pass made by the opponent, or intervene in cases where the striker has got past a defender who was contrasting the ball. A player who is covering 'the ball' must place himself inside the cone which, as we have already seen, has as its apex the player in possession and as its base the goal posts (Fig 18). Often, however, it is enough to take up a position from which you will be able to close in on the player in possession if he manages to get past his direct adversary (Fig. 19).

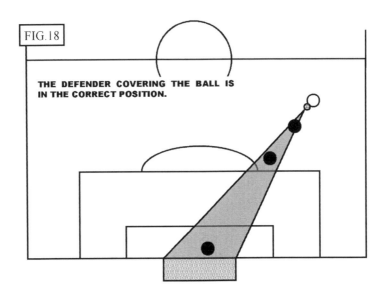

FIG.18

THE DEFENDER COVERING THE BALL IS
IN THE CORRECT POSITION.

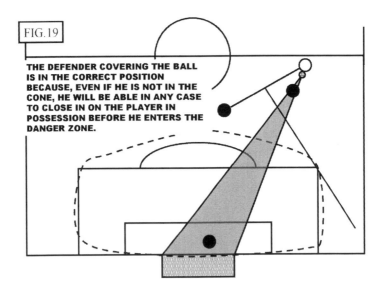

FIG.19

THE DEFENDER COVERING THE BALL
IS IN THE CORRECT POSITION
BECAUSE, EVEN IF HE IS NOT IN THE
CONE, HE WILL BE ABLE IN ANY CASE
TO CLOSE IN ON THE PLAYER IN
POSSESSION BEFORE HE ENTERS THE
DANGER ZONE.

40

The distance separating the defender in coverage from the player in possession will vary in relation to the stretch of field between the striker and the goal. As we already saw when speaking about 'T' marking, it is important for the defender in coverage to be able to contrast his opponent before he enters the 'danger zone', i.e., that part of the field from which it will be possible for him to have a good shot at goal. In a nutshell. the closer the striker is to the goal the nearer to him the defender covering him should be.

When a player must place himself to mark an opponent as well as being ready to go in coverage, then he must be able to put himself in the right position. The defender has a double role, and it is important to see if he can place himself in such a way as to allow him to close in on the opponent in possession and on his direct adversary in case he should receive a pass.

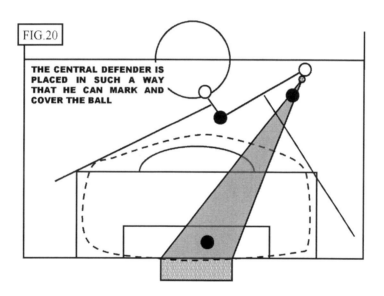

FIG.20

THE CENTRAL DEFENDER IS PLACED IN SUCH A WAY THAT HE CAN MARK AND COVER THE BALL

If, on account of the situation on the field, it is impossible to take up a position that will allow you to carry out both these functions, you will have to see if there is a team mate who can help in marking. It often happens that a team mate of the same section, continuing to mark his direct opponent, takes up a position that will allow him if necessary to close in on the adversary normally marked by another player, now occupied in coverage. In order to see if such a possibility exists, theoretically at least, we would have to define the closing lines of the various defenders and verify if they interconnect outside the danger zone (Fig. 21).

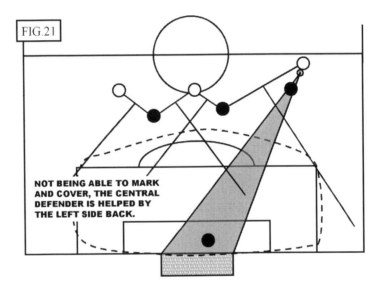

FIG.21

NOT BEING ABLE TO MARK
AND COVER, THE CENTRAL
DEFENDER IS HELPED BY
THE LEFT SIDE BACK.

If there is no team mate who can help you with marking, then you must wait, concentrate on marking and close in on the ball only when the striker has got past the player who should have been guaranteeing coverage.

It goes without saying that the player on the field will not be able to make all these considerations in an instant, and he will be guided by his instinct. The coach's job during training sessions will be to supply the single player with all necessary technical and tactical know-how that will permit him to act for the best.

Having now had a look at how to cover 'the ball' let us now go on to survey the important tactical aspects regarding coverage of space.

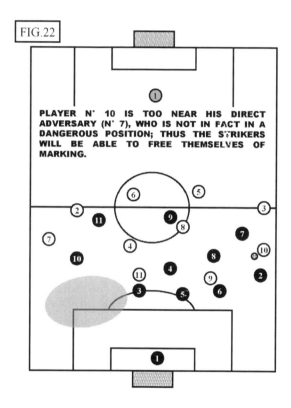

FIG.22

PLAYER N° 10 IS TOO NEAR HIS DIRECT ADVERSARY (N° 7), WHO IS NOT IN FACT IN A DANGEROUS POSITION; THUS THE STRIKERS WILL BE ABLE TO FREE THEMSELVES OF MARKING.

What we are talking about here is the intelligent placement of a player trying to regain possession. Having no opponent in a dangerous position, he will be able to cover a certain part of the field (Fig. 22 and 23).

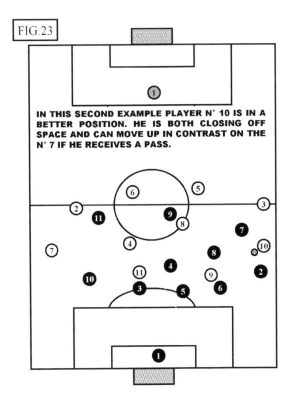

FIG.23

IN THIS SECOND EXAMPLE PLAYER N° 10 IS IN A BETTER POSITION. HE IS BOTH CLOSING OFF SPACE AND CAN MOVE UP IN CONTRAST ON THE N° 7 IF HE RECEIVES A PASS.

When a defender covers a portion of the field this gives us a double advantage: it allows his team mates to bring themselves closer to the ball, reducing the opponents' space and playing time, and at the same time, by placing himself in such a way, the player is taking away a part of the field that a rival striker could otherwise use to free himself of marking.

CHAPTER 4

PRESSING IN THE ATTACKING ZONE

ULTRA-OFFENSIVE PRESSING

In order for ultra-offensive pressing to be really effective the whole team must participate in it, strikers included. It stands to reason that in the very moment the team loses ball possession and switches to the defense phase, the players will not be in the right positions to carry out organized pressing; but this disadvantage is compensated for by the simple fact that the opponents will not be organized either to develop their attacking moves at once. If we carry out immediate individual pressing on the player in possession this will have the effect of slowing down their attacking play, which in turn will permit our team to get back into the right position. However, by putting pressure on the player in possession, we might stimulate him into playing the ball forwards more quickly, not giving us the time to get into place. In other words, if the opponent who has regained possession is able to read the situation quickly and put his team into an instant counterattack, then our attempt to put him under imme-diate pressure is just a way of encouraging him to speed up his counterattack. If, on the other hand, the player who has regained possession is slow, is not used to or is not able to switch immediate-ly into the attacking phase, then, by putting immediate pressure on him, we are succeeding in our aim to slow down our adversary's attacking play. In order to judge a player's ability to move into attack, we should keep in mind not only his particular strengths and weak-nesses, but also the general context in which he finds himself (part of the field, position of his body, etc.).

Offensive pressing, or, more correctly, immediate pressing in the attacking zone, is based on *the team's ability to close in on the player in pos-session, on the players to whom he can pass and on his players in support*, more than on our ability to create situations of numerical superiority. A player who finds himself in possession in his own half will clearly feel under greater pressure not to lose the ball than a player who is playing it in or around his opponent's area. This means that the player in his own half will have fewer useful or intelligent moves open to him (in cases like this, for example, dribbling an opponent will become a risky move and something to be avoided), and he will be trying to avoid losing ball possession rather than set up attacking plays. Normally, therefore, when a player with the ball is under pressure in this part of the field, he will attempt to make a long pass. All this considered, if we want to carry out immediate pressing we must:

- put the player in possession under pressure;
- cut the player in possession off as quickly as we can from his possible passing lines (dumps or passes to a supporting player);
- be ready to cover any in-depth supporting players to whom he might make a long pass.

PRESSING IN THE ATTACKING ZONE

We have to decide whether pressing in the attacking zone should be carried out all through the match or only in certain cases. In the first case, it is the coach's own philosophy which determines the team's defense strategy, while in the second the team is merely aligning its tactical behavior to certain accidental factors – we are losing, the team is in numerical superiority and wants to win, there is not much time left and we have to unlock the result and so on – which will condition and modify our original strategy.

Before we make a closer analysis of the tactics and the characteristics of pressing in the offense zone, we must make an elementary point: there are, of course, enormous differences between offensive and defensive pressing.

Looking at the tactical behavior of soccer teams, one of the things we will always notice is *the fairly static and clear cut placement of the defenders*, who tend to move along pre-established lines. In the attacking zone, on the contrary, the strikers try to move along the whole front with the mid fielders inserting themselves as well. This creates a situation of great dynamism, which makes it difficult for those who are trying to defend to establish precise points of reference. This is taking place for obvious tactical reasons: the defense section is usually playing in numerical superiority over the opposition's attacking group, so that all they need to do is to pass the ball correctly in order to gain depth and field. Secondly, all the activity that takes place in the attacking zone would not be feasible in defense because of the risks you would be running if you lost possession (and in such an event the team would have great difficulty in getting back into order). It must also be added that great vitality is required of the players in the offensive zone, in particular when the team is facing a well-drawn up defense that is also playing in numerical superiority.

All this goes to show us that it is easier to give precise points of reference to be 'attacked' in the offense, rather than in the defense, zone.

Naturally, this advantage is offset by the fact that if you want to use pressing in the attacking zone, then the ball must be in that part of the field; and that, in turn, does not depend wholly on our ability to keep the team tight and compact with the defense line drawn up in or around the mid field line. If the adversaries attempt to override the mid fielders by the continuous and systematic use of long passes, that will complicate our application of offensive pressing.

Besides this, however, in order to use good ultra offensive pressing, the team must be good at the rebound so that it can maintain depth, and, above all, the players must be able to handle negative transition (the passage from a situation of possession to the defense phase) so that they can immediately crush their adversaries' attempts to organize their plays.

We have already seen that more than doubling up on the player in possession, (who, in any case, on account of the zone in which he is working, will have to reduce the range of plays open to him) *the important thing for the team is the crispness of its tempo as it goes into pressure.* When one man goes into pressure on the player in possession, his team mates must close in on the rival players to whom the ball could be passed (supporting players that are near or far away and any other players that might be useful). The real problem about organizing helpful pressing in the attacking zone is connected with giving the team *working time in common.* One way of hiding any possible problems there might be in its tempo is to make sure the team can defend itself using all its men and with *the maximum aggressiveness in all the zones of the field.* Putting your opponents under the maximum pressure means, in fact, (apart from forcing them to play at your own rhythm), slowing down the general tempo of their plays, on both an individual and a collective level, which will be to our advantage in that we will have more time for our shifting moves and will be able to get back into our places before it is too late.

To sum up we can say that the most important factors underlying good offensive pressing are:

- the team's ability to work together;
- speed during negative transition and in adapting to the various tactical situations on the field;
- aggressiveness.

From a strategic point of view, what we need in order to organize prompt and remunerative pressing in the attacking zone is to 'shape' our placement in relation to the tactical system being used by our opponents. In particular, it is important:

- analyze the number of components in the defense line;
- study the movements and the openings the opposing defense section will be looking for so as to line up our own team with the system that will make it easiest for us systematically to close off 'the playing solutions' open to the defenders who have gained possession.

If, for example, we are facing an adversary lined up with a 4-4-3, the best way to press in the attacking zone will be to close off the players' passing lines as shown in Fig. 24.

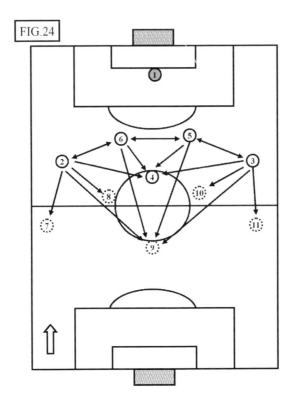

FIG.24

The side backs (essential points of reference on whom the center players will be depending to keep the ball on the move) and the center mid fielder (all important apex in the team's building up plays) will be the players who we will have to be most careful about. Apart from identifying which men to press, our players will have to be clear about which passing lines to close off in order to make their opponent's building up maneuvers as difficult as possible. For example, with the left side back N° 2 in possession, the opposing players to be shut off are:

- the supporting center back (N° 6);
- the mid fielders waiting to take the ball on the inside (N° 8 and 4);
- the right wing (N° 7) on the sidelines;
- the center forward (N° 9), who is acting as an advanced point of reference in the center.

As far as defensive pressing is concerned, and in order to create the density of manpower that will allow us to double up on opposing players, it is important to know what type of movements the strikers will carry out to free themselves of marking, and the directions in which the mid fielders are going to insert themselves. When we intend to use pressing in the attacking zone it becomes of absolutely fundamental importance to *define our adversary's points of reference during the build up phase and the passing lines that we will have to cover.*

To return to the preceding example, in which we were having a look at a team lined up with the 4-4-3: here is a proposal for good pressing in the attacking zone.

Remember that it is easier to carry out pressing on the sidelines (for reasons that we have already explained in Chapter 1). It is important, therefore, that we 'encourage' our opponents to pass the ball in such a way that it finishes up with the side backs. Once the ball has come into their possession, we must put them under individual pressure. Our player, whose job it is to close off this point of reference, must make his move as soon as he gets the feeling that the ball is on the point of arriving to his direct opponents. He must not wait until his adversary has stopped and controlled the ball, but must go into pressure before this happens. At the same time, the team must be able to close off the passing lines shown in Fig. 24 (passing along the sidelines to the wing, short pass to cut to the side mid fielder, diagonal pass to center mid fielder, dump on the center defender, long pass to the center forward).

Linked to all this, the coach's job will be the attempt to find the best formula (or tactical lineup) to make sure that the team can carry out the closing up plays that we have already illustrated *as quickly as possible*. Speaking practically, the coach must try to place his men in such a way that they will be able to find the opposition's point of view in a natural way without having to carry out movements (or shifts) that will be too long – that, of course, would complicate the work of the individuals and as a consequence the operations of the collective whole.

We will now give three examples of ultra-offensive pressing carried out with three different playing systems (the 3-5-2, the 4-4-2 and the 4-2-3-1).

When we are playing with the 3-5-2, and face a 4-3-3 we get the following tactical situation: in the mid field both sections are drawn up with a low apex (center mid fielder); on the sidelines the side backs of the 4-3-3 will be doing most of the work carried out instead by the side mid fielders of the 3-5-2; the two center backs of the 4-3-3 will be coping with the two center strikers of the 3-5-2; and the three-man attack of the 4-3-3 will be faced by the three defenders of the 3-5-2. The situation is clearly illustrated in Fig. 25, and it will be very difficult for the 3-5-2 to create attacking pressing.

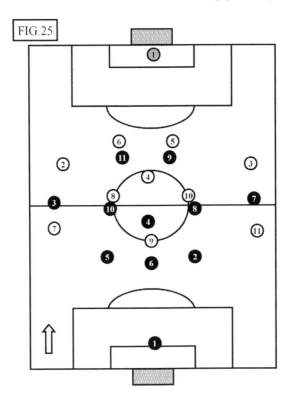

FIG.25

In passing the ball at the level of the defense line we have a clear situation of 4 (defenders) against 3 (strikers) in favor of the defense section of the 4-3-3. This will create problems in closing in quickly on the side backs of the 4-3-3. To shut them off we can bring one of the strikers wide (while the other cuts off his possibility of dumping the ball), or we could bring a side mid fielder into depth. Neither of these solutions is particularly good however, for the sim-

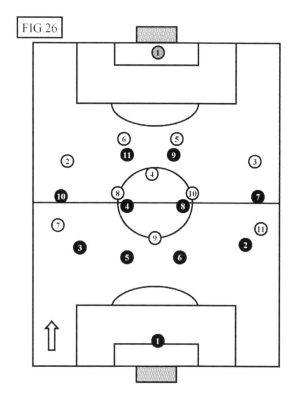

FIG.26

ple reason that the striker running wide or the mid fielder coming into depth will have to cover quite a lot of ground before reaching the player in possession (or what we call 'the closing point').

In theory, we could also bring the side mid fielders of the 3-5-2 forward to improve the situation, transforming the initial system into a reckless 3-3-4.

We should keep a second problem in mind, however, in connection with the face off of the two teams in the mid field.

As we have already seen, both teams have placed their players in such a way as to form a triangle with its apex towards the back. For this reason the players will find it difficult to time their play when they are moving in against the opposing center mid fielder.

A possible solution might be to place the strikers in a vertical formation, with the first striker closing off the dumping pass, and the second covering the center mid fielder.

Even this solution has its disadvantages, in particular when the 4-4-3 is facing a 4-4-2. If we make a tactical analysis of Fig. 26 it will be clear that the three-man attack of the 4-3-3 is facing the four-man defense of the 4-3-3. In the mid field, the four mid field players of the 4-4-2 – as against the three mid fielders of the 4-3-3 – will give them only apparent numerical superiority, because the side players of the 4-4-2 will have their work cut out with the in-depth movements of the 4-3-3's side backs; the fact being that the 4-3-3 will have operative numerical superiority in the central zone with respect to the two side players of the 4-4-2.

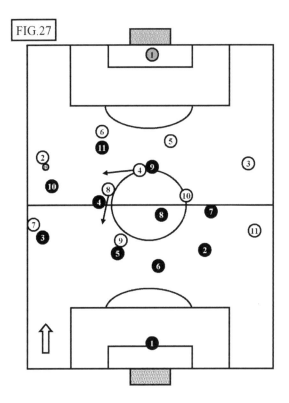

FIG.27

If, instead of a 4-3-3, we are facing a 4-2-3-1, as shown in Fig. 28, then the distances and the placement of the players give us the chance to exploit pressing in the attacking zone to the top. In this case the players are already 'in the right positions' and it will be much easier for them to put individual pressure on their opponents.

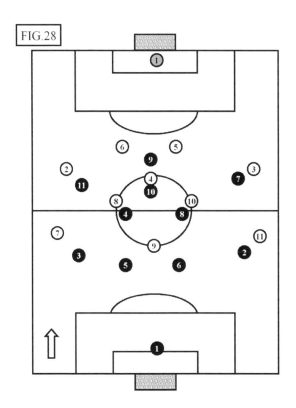

CHAPTER 5

EXERCISES

EXERCISES

Effective pressing requires that the players go to create numerical superiority or positive numerical density in or around the ball zone. In order to get more players into the ball zone than the adversaries, the team needs to be on the move, going in to occupy (or 'block') the parts of the field near the opposing player in possession. Keeping in mind, however, that the ball can 'travel' faster than any player, first of all, and, secondly, that in order to converge on the ball zone, the team will be leaving parts of the field free on the weak side – you will see how important it is to avoid giving the opponents a chance to make a quick change of front, or, if they do, to make sure that we are not completely unprepared.

In order to get the most out of their pressing, the team must be good at directing their opponent's maneuvers, forcing them to play in a pre-established area of the field. Naturally, once the adversaries have been 'put' where we want them to be, the quality of our pressing is also important.

In order to get to the point where the team is capable of carrying out organized pressing with good tempo, we have to follow things on both an individual and a collective level. It is important also to react to the quality of the play and to the system used by the opponents we are about to face, making little adjustments to our basic procedures so as to facilitate our players' tasks, which in turn will give us more results from our pressing. Without considering the particular system that we are using, there is a difference between pressing an opponent lined up with a 4-3-3, let us say, and another lined up with a 4-4-2. The distances between our players and the opponents they are referring to will be different, as will the situations of numerical superiority, equality or inferiority in the various parts of the playing field.

The exercises we will be proposing in the following pages keep in mind the following factors:

1) individual ability:

- skills in playing 1 against 1
- taking up a dynamic position

2) collective organization:

- doubling up skills
- covering skills
- position when waiting for an uncovered ball
- aggressive position on a covered ball

In the two appendixes relative to *offside* and *going into counter attack* specific exercises will be presented in connection to these two aspects of play, which are so closely connected with pressing.

INDIVIDUAL EXERCISES

Individual exercises are of fundamental importance in underlining the team's tactical plan. The single player must be able to diversify the pressure he is putting on his opponent in relation to both the global tactical context and the placement of the direct adversary (not only in terms of how near or far away he is from the goal but also in reference to the position of his body – in front / behind / sideways). The single player must then be able quickly to take up the best possible position with regard to the tactical task that he has to carry out. All this must be taking place with verve and perfect tempo because, in order to be as effective as possible, all this shifting of position must be as closely connected as possible to the development of the opponent's plays and the changes in the tactical context.

As far as the individual player is concerned, the most important things to improve are his ability to contrast an opponent with the ball (1 to 1 duel) and his competence in placing himself correctly when it is his job to control and mark an adversary who is not actually in possession.

BUILDING UP A PLAYER'S DEFENSE TECHNIQUES WHEN HIS TASK IS TO CONTRAST AN OPPONENT IN POSSESSION

The following are the most important skills as regards a defender who is contrasting a player in possession

- *ability in anticipation.* The defender is able to read fore see and anticipate his opponent's intentions;
- *ability to position himself correctly.* The defender man ages to take up a position which – as far as distance and body posture are concerned – will allow him to move in an effective way whatever direction his opponent takes with the ball. It is vital not to arrive in front of your adversary when you are off-balance, or with mistaken timing;
- *ability in forcing.* The defender is able to 'tune himself' with the striker, placing himself along the trajectory followed by the opponent in possession (which is normally the line going from the ball to the goal). In this way he obliges his man to direct himself towards less dangerous zones (towards the sidelines) or to move the ball onto his weaker foot;
- *contrasting techniques.* The defender intervenes against the opponent with perfect timing and technique. In this sense, we should remember that, in order to make the most of his intervention, it is a good idea that the defender should keep his eye on the ball, that he should shorten his steps as he gets ready to carry out the contrast in order to gain in his ability to respond, that his body weight is well distributed both on his supporting foot and on that which is about to intervene, and that the power of the foot that actually carries out the contrast should be directed towards the center of the ball.

60

Here is a list of the types of contrasts that the defender might be expected to carry out:

- *frontal contrast.* In these cases the defender must intervene with the inside of the foot which is nearest to the ball. At the same time his body balance must be lower than usual;
- *side contrast.* This type of contrast is carried out when the opponent in possession is moving forward with the defender at his side. It is important in these cases that, once the defender had got himself into a good position, with his supporting foot in line with, or, even better, just in front of the ball, he should swivel round on the supporting foot as he goes into contrast with the other. It is possible to intervene on the ball with the inside of the foot furthest from striker, or with the outside of the foot nearest to your man;
- *sliding contrast.* Another type of contrast is the sliding tackle, which corresponds to the technical factors that we have already seen. In this case, however, the defender will have to judge whether this intervention is really necessary. If it should fail or turn out to be ineffective, the defender will very probably be unable to rectify the situation;
- *contrasting with your opponent behind you.* In this situation the defender is behind the striker. It is important here that the back should not be too near the player in possession so that the striker cannot support himself and swivel around on the defender using his arms and body. The striker should not be fully aware of the defender's position, and, if anything, it should be the back himself who will put his hand on the striker to make sure he does not come too close. There are two good or possible moments for the actual intervention. The first is immediately after the striker has taken control of the ball. His play might not be perfect, or could leave margins which will allow a sharp or attentive defender to carry out a positive contrast. Another favorable moment for the intervention is when the striker is trying to turn. In moments like this the ball will not be correctly defended and the opponent will probably not be in perfect balance, with

most of his body weight falling on his supporting foot. In this case the defender will probably be able to intervene with success if he is placed at the right distance.

EXERCISE 1: ONE AGAINST ONE FROM DIFFERENT DIRECTIONS

Three defenders are placed on the sides of the rectangle shown in Fig. 29. The striker in possession arrives from the free side. As soon as he is about to enter the area of play, the coach will call one of the defenders, who will have to stop the striker from bringing the ball over the line from which the defender has come. This exercise stimulates the defender's ability to take up position in relation to where the striker is arriving from (side or frontal contrast).

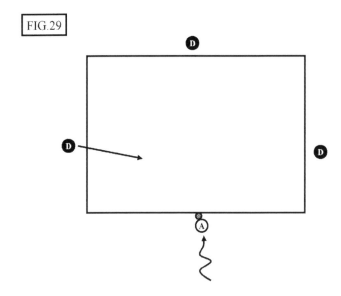

FIG.29

EXERCISE 2: ONE AGAINST ONE WITH GOALS THAT ARE NOT ALIGNED

Two players placed one in front of the other are trying to get past each other to score a goal. It is important that the goals should not be aligned so as to create a strong and a weak side, and to encourage the defender to force his opponent into the side of the field furthest away from the goal that he is defending. Fig. 30 is a detailed illustration of the exercise.

FIG.30

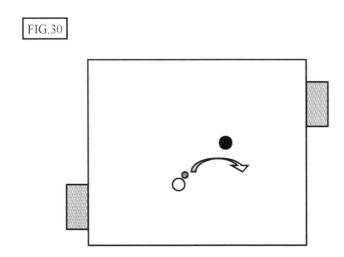

EXERCISE 3: ONE AGAINST ONE WITH TWO GOALS

The striker in possession goes straight towards the defender, who must be good at forcing his opponent to switch the ball onto his weak foot.

FIG.31

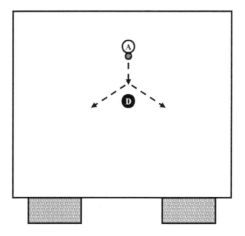

EXERCISE 4: ONE AGAINST ONE WITH GOALKEEPERS

Two players face each other one against one. Their purpose is to stop the opponent from shooting dangerously at the goal defended by the keepers. You can organize the exercise in such a way that one player will be attacking while the other is defending, or you can make them play without interruption so that each player can switch from being a defender to being a striker depending on the situation. It is important to make clear that the goalkeeper must only defend his goal and cannot support his companion's plays in any way.
The figure below is an illustration of the exercise.

FIG.32

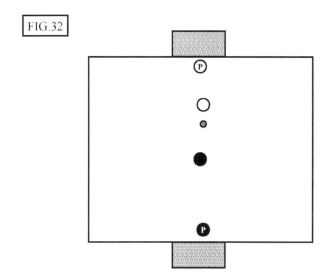

EXERCISE 5: ONE AGAINST ONE FROM THE SIDE

Two defenders are placed at the side of the rectangle shown in the figure, while there are two small goals on the side opposite to the one from which the striker is moving. The coach will call a defender as soon as the striker is about to enter the playing area, and it will be his job to defend whichever of the two goals has been decided on before. This exercise helps to improve the individual's ability in side contrasts.

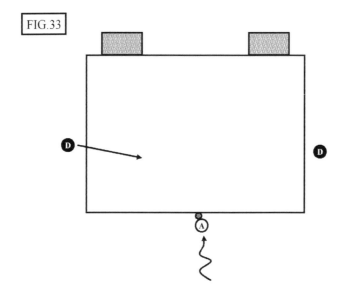

FIG.33

EXERCISE 6: ONE AGAINST ONE FROM THE SIDE WITH A GOALKEEPER

In this situation we have a face off between the attacking player, whose aim it is to score, and the defender, who is arriving from the side. The purpose of the exercise is to improve the defender's side contrast, making sure that the striker with the ball cannot get forward in the direction he was going and has to shoot from another less central position.

You can change the defenders' starting point so as to vary the angle at which he will be running in his approach to the attacking player.

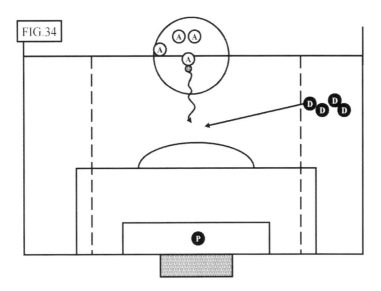

FIG.34

EXERCISE 7: ONE AGAINST ONE FROM BEHIND

The defender must contrast the attacking player, who, as he receives the ball from the coach has to turn and shoot on goal.
The aim of this exercise is to improve defending technique when the attacking player has his back to the defender.

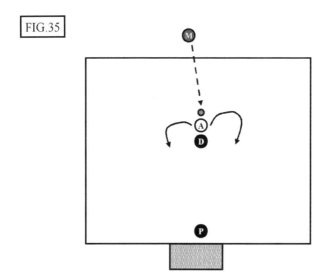

FIG.35

EXERCISE 8: ONE AGAINST ONE FROM BEHIND

Inside a rectangle marked out on the field, the attacking player receives a ball from the coach and has to hold on to it as long as possible. The defender must try to regain possession, or, in any case, intervene, forcing the striker out of line. The difference from the last exercise, where the defender was making sure that the attacking player could not turn round and shoot at goal, is that in this new situation the defender will be concentrating only on his contrasting techniques.

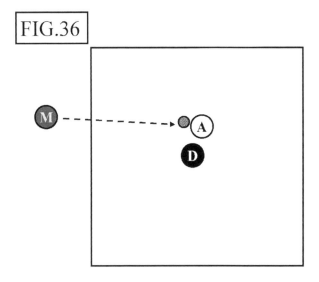

FIG.36

EXERCISE 9: ONE AGAINST ONE TRYING TO GET BACK ADVANTAGE

The attacking player takes the ball from the lower circumference of the mid field circle. He will be followed by the defender starting out from the disc at the center of the field. This is a useful exercise for improving slip-in tackles and getting back advantage.

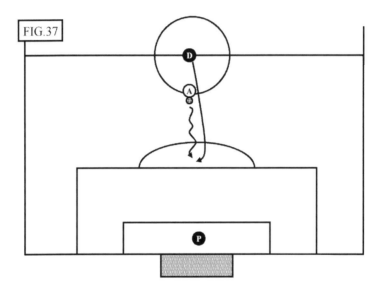

EXERCISE 10: TWO AGAINST TWO IN PRE-ESTABLISHED SECTORS

The exercise we now propose sums up all the specific techniques drilled by the particular procedures we have been using previously. Here, two attacking players are opposed to two defenders. Each group of four players is not allowed to go over the mid field line, and what we are talking about is a special training match with the strikers intent on getting by the defenders in order to shoot at goal. Each defender will have a striker to cover, and team mates or attacking players will not be allowed to help by moving backwards - because in this exercise we want to concentrate on marking. We must note, however, that here the individual duels are more closely connected with the reality of the playing field because the strikers can pass to a team mate as well as dump on his defenders. The limits of the previous, more single-minded exercises are that the striker will be obliged to use dribbling alone, making it easier for the back to concentrate exclusively on his defense techniques.

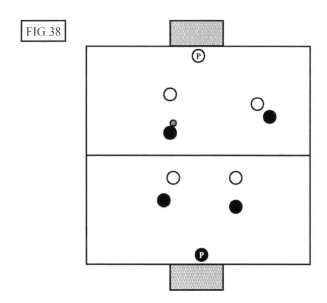

FIG.38

BUILDING UP THE DEFENDER'S ABILITY IN DEFENSE
TECHNIQUES WHEN THE PLAYER HAS TO CONTROL AN
OPPONENT WITHOUT THE BALL

When a player is not directly involved in controlling an opponent in
possession he will be doing one of the following two things:

- marking a striker who is not in possessions;
- tactical work (covering; getting back; doubling up)

Concerning marking the opponent without the ball, it is essential
that the defender knows how to place himself in the best position
from which to see both *the opponent in possession and his direct adversary.*
In order to mark out the best position to take up, defenders make
an imaginary triangle (as shown in the figure) which has, as its three
angles, the opponent in possession, the direct adversary and the center of the goal.

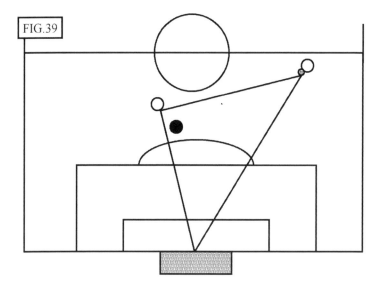

We can say that the defender is in the right position if he is inside
the triangle and placed in such a way to impede his opponent from
receiving the ball in-depth, while at the same time being able to make an
attempt *to anticipate the ball* while it is traveling towards the striker.

72

The distance that the marker has to keep from his opponent will vary (increase) depending *how far away the striker is from the ball zone*. In particular, when we are talking about supporting players around the ball, he must shorten up this distance to an arm's length from the attacking player, and it is important as well that the defender keeps himself ready and on his marks, with his knees and ankles bent and his eyes in the direction of both the striker to be marked and the line across which the ball will be passed.

EXERCISE 1: ONE AGAINST ONE WITH DUMP AND REBOUND PASSES

The defender must continually change his position in reference to the movements of the ball. The supporting players (dumps) cannot abandon the positions that have been assigned to them, while the attacking player who the defender is covering can play all over the offensive front.

The three players in position (dumps) will have to exchange the ball as quickly as possible looking as frequently as they can for the center striker, who will be able to use their support in his attempts to get into depth and try to shoot at goal.

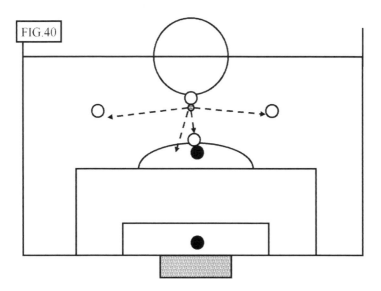

EXERCISE 2: ONE AGAINST ONE DURING A CROSS

This exercise follows the same procedures as the last, but this time there are an extra two players in position on the field ready to cross from the sides.

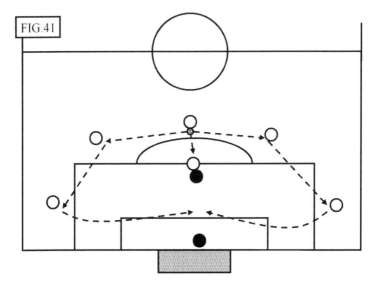

EXERCISE 3: ONE AGAINST ONE IN A MATCH SITUATION

This exercise foresees a match to be played by fixed couples. Each player has a specific opponent to control in the defense phase and to get by in offense. Play is developed by free touches and in cases where a striker gets past his direct opponent none of the other defenders can intervene. When, on the other hand, the defender manages to intercept a ball he turns into a striker and will be contrasted only by his direct opponent trying to get back advantage on him.

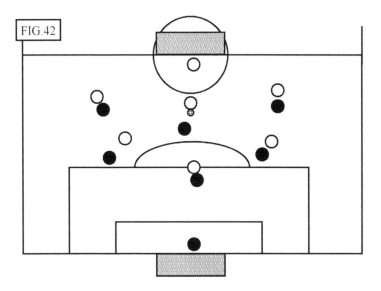

FIG.42

EXERCISE 4: TEACHING HOW TO COVER

There are many exercises suitable for training how to take up a position in coverage of a team mate who has gone out in pressure on the ball:

- a line of three or four attacks points of reference on the field – cones or the diagonal lines between them;
- a line of three or four attack the ball being passed horizontally from one team mate to another.

Here is a useful suggestion for training players' speed in movement. Four strikers are lined up along the same row 15 – 20 yards outside the penalty area, and they are passing the ball quickly to each other. The four defenders in front of them have to try to follow the movement of the ball in a horizontal direction. When the coach blows the whistle, the striker in possession will have to make a vertical dash through the line of defenders, ending up with a shot on goal. It will be the task of the defender or the defenders covering him to go in contrast, not the player who happens to find himself in front.

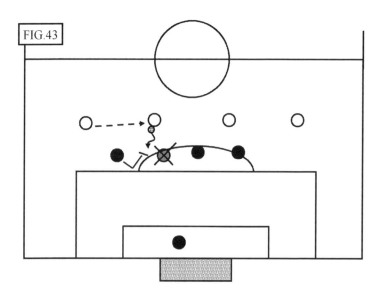

FIG.43

EXERCISE 5: TEACHING DOUBLING UP

Using the following exercise we can introduce the players to the basics of collective tactics. In the rectangle the four players placed in the corners exchange the ball by passing along the sidelines. The defenders alternate between putting pressure on the players and positioning themselves in coverage. When the coach gives the sign the striker in possession brings the ball to the team mate in front of him, with the defenders running in to double up.

FIG.44

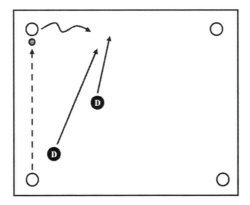

EXERCISE 6: TEACHING HORIZONTAL DOUBLING UP

The three white players pass the ball around, with the defenders moving in relation to the movements of the ball. At the coach's whistle the striker in possession will have to bring the ball over the marked line. Moving towards the strong side the defenders will bring two players to double up on the player in possession.

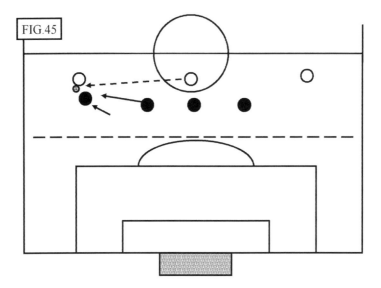

FIG.45

EXERCISE 7: TEACHING DOUBLING UP IN A BACKWARD MOVEMENT

This exercise is similar to the last. By adding a second line of strikers, we are training the defenders to carry out doubling up as they move backwards. Once they have received the ball, the strikers must try to get past the men marking them directly, and try to shoot at goal. The team involved in the defense phase must attempt to regain possession by good doubling up moves. As the examples show, we can double up on the strikers in various different ways. Match by match, we can choose different solutions depending on our own or the opponent's characteristics, and on the placement of the players depending on the tactical system used by the teams.

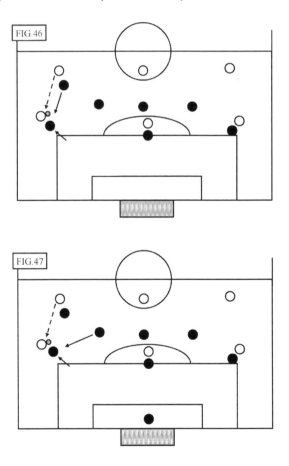

EXERCISE 8: A PRESSING TRAINING MATCH

The four players in the central zone pass the ball to each other with the opponents putting them under pressure so that they cannot pass the ball vertically onto the strikers. The defenders cannot gain possession except by intercepting a forward pass. Once the strikers have received a ball filtering through from a team mate they can shoot. Apart from undergoing pressure from their direct marker, they will also have to free themselves of the mid fielder moving back to double up as shown in the figure.

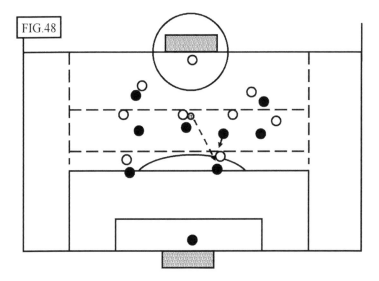

FIG.48

COLLECTIVE EXERCISES

When the players have acquired good individual skills we can move on to teach them how to carry out real pressing. The coach will choose the type of pressing he wants to implement, depending on his players' characteristics and on his own philosophy of play, and, on this basis, he will prepare the most suitable teaching methods to demonstrate their tasks to his players, and to show them the movements they must carry out.

Here, we will take a marginal look at this build up instruction, because it is something that will have to be adapted to the type of pressing and the ideas of the coach.

In short, we can say that with these exercises the coach will be trying to:

- make sure that each single section understands the movements to be carried out;
- coordinate the movements of the various sections so that he gets a team playing as a block

What we will be suggesting in this section are a number of exercises that will improve the coordination and the timing of the team.

No matter what type of pressing you are implementing, the basic aim is that the timing of the team's movements must be homogenous.

A team can know the movements to be carried out by heart; but if they do not apply them with a precise sense of timing, their pressing will be absolutely ineffective.

The essential factors that will turn your pressing into an extraordinary weapon in the defense phase are as follows:

- good individual defense skills;
- perfect grasp of the collective mechanisms;
- precision and timing in the application of pressing;
- competitive aggressiveness.

EXERCISE 1

Inside a square three defenders and five strikers are placed as in the figure (one of the strikers in the center with good freedom of movement and the others in the corners). The strikers pass the ball around, and the defenders will be expected to refine the timing of their group pressing.

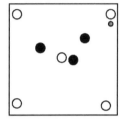

EXERCISE 2

Four defenders and two strikers interact inside a square. Four other attacking players are placed outside the square along the lines. The players outside the square are allowed only two touches while the players on the inside can do what they want. The attacking players are to carry out an established number of passes, whereas the defender's job is to intercept the ball.

This exercise helps the defenders to get into the habit of moving in a coordinated way and with the right timing in order to close off the lines by which the strikers will be passing to each other.

FIG.50

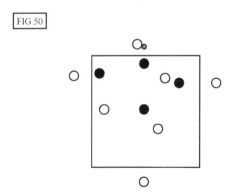

82

EXERCISE 3:

The whole team (in black) is placed on the full playing field. They have to move about following the motion of the ball which the opponents (in white) will be passing around keeping to their positions (Fig. 51). When the coach gives the signal the player in possession has to set up a real attacking play. At this point the defenders, who have been simulating up to now, will then begin to press in earnest.

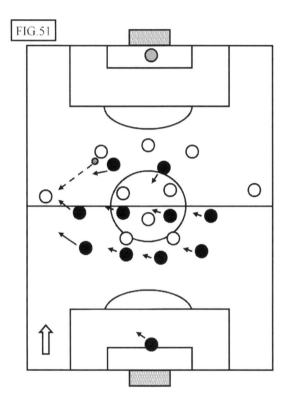

FIG.51

CHAPTER 6

PRESSING AND MENTALITY

Successful pressing requires that *the players believe in what they are doing*. Pressing is not only physically, but also mentally tiring; and without results that reward the efforts of the team it will certainly be difficult for the coach to convince his group of just how good his ideas and directives really are.

Why should a player run back and forwards like crazy just to gain possession, and how can the coach convince him of the necessity of all this exertion?

If the coach is to be credible and to hold onto the trust of his group he must persist with the type of soccer in which he believes without having any apparent second thoughts.

Only a coach who is sure of himself and of that which he is proposing can convince the team to use the methods which he is setting forth.

Apart from this preliminary consideration, it goes without saying that for pressing to be effective the whole team must be motivated and ready to carry it into effect.

Clearly, the teaching method used will depend on the type of pressing the coach wants the team to carry out; but we could say the very same thing about the strategy he employs in motivating his team. It is easier to explain the tactical reasons for moving backwards in order to double up in the defense phase than to account for the fact that a striker who has just lost possession must move out and follow his opposing defender. General tactical explanations may be convincing enough to get the team to press in defense, but you will have to come up with very good reasons to make them press in the attacking zone whether the team is winning or losing.

In cases like these the coach must be very good at 'selling' his project to the players, and may even need the club's support above all at the beginning, when the team's progress, the improvement in its play and the results might still be subject to fluctuation.

Nevertheless, it is always better to convince the players and the team as a whole of the necessity of carrying out certain movements and running certain risks rather than attempting to impose your ideas on them by force.

It is much more effective – though, of course also more complicated – if you can convince people of the value of your beliefs by showing them the worth of your ideas rather than by simply exploiting your role (the coach) as a sort of pre-appointed guide.

However, the coach that is putting his personal convictions on the line in order to create play for his team must not forget that his role gives him more responsibility than that of a simple player, and if he has an open attitude towards the team this does not de-legitimize his position.

It is a good thing, in order to give the team the motivation they will need if they are to apply pressing on the whole field, for the coach to explain the advantages and the value of the project (reasoning with them or giving them real or statistical information about this type of play). It may even have a positive effect if the coach tells his team that he has doubts about their ability to do the things in which he believes. A concrete obstacle must be set before the players if we are to create a challenging situation for them.

This little dodge will also mean that the first difficulties that arrive can be justified by the coach saying that the doubts which he had already set forth to the team have now come true. All this, apart from further underlining the challenge in itself and stimulating the players' pride, will also strengthen the coach's position. The force of his project will not have been undermined and, having foreseen everything, he will now have the reputation of being a sort of 'clairvoyant'.

By looking after every detail and correcting errors or individual shortcomings, he will be able to motivate the players by underlining the collective nature of the project and arguing that, for the very reason that they are all part of a team, each single player must follow the directives with tenacity and all-out dedication in order to arrive at the common aim.

Doing all he can to create the right mentality, the coach will have to stress and praise the team as often as he can for the progress they are making. He will also have to take the group to task as well whenever he feels that they are resting on their laurels.

Another important thing for the creation of group mentality is to teach your players to communicate with each other on the field. Short and decisive words like 'yours', 'mine', 'my block', 'change', 'go', 'leave it', 'coming', 'run' etc., apart from simplifying the tactical work of the individual, will also make it easy for them to acquire tactical skills and mentality.

I am of the firm opinion, however, that in order to get the team to play the type of soccer that you have in mind, what you have to get across to the group is the feeling of a challenge to be overcome or the dream to make come true, while at the same time you are stirring up their pride as players.

A team that has a mission to accomplish and which has to bring out everything they have inside to reach their objective, will, without any doubt, be at an advantage over one which is blindly trying to follow the coach's own project.

To sum up we must underline it once again: you will never be able to carry out effective pressing if you do not have the right mentality in the defense phase.

APPENDIX 1

OFFSIDE

WHEN IS THE STRIKER OFFSIDE?

A player is in an offside position (and by rights he will have a free kick given against him when he receives the ball) if he does not have at least two opponents placed nearer to the base line than he is. The offside position can be considered passive, and therefore not punishable, in cases where the player is not actively participating in the action or if he is in a part of the field so out of the way as not to influence the regular development of play.

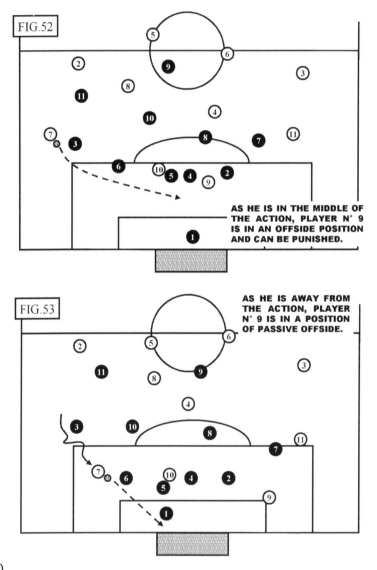

FIG.52

AS HE IS IN THE MIDDLE OF THE ACTION, PLAYER N° 9 IS IN AN OFFSIDE POSITION AND CAN BE PUNISHED.

AS HE IS AWAY FROM THE ACTION, PLAYER N° 9 IS IN A POSITION OF PASSIVE OFFSIDE.

FIG.53

A DEFINITION OF TACTICAL OFFSIDE

Tactical offside is when the defense section moves up in such a way as to put the opposing strikers in an irregular position. More precisely, we call it *active offside* when the defense section or the defense line moves into depth with the purpose of putting the attacking player in an irregular position. We speak about tactics of *passive offside* when it is the attacking player who himself assumes an irregular position in relation to the defense line.

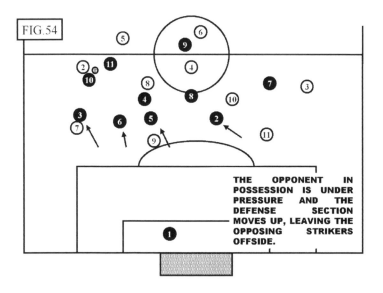

FIG.54

THE OPPONENT IN POSSESSION IS UNDER PRESSURE AND THE DEFENSE SECTION MOVES UP, LEAVING THE OPPOSING STRIKERS OFFSIDE.

WHEN YOU NEED TO APPLY OFFSIDE TACTICS

The first thing to say is that offside tactics are a way of regaining possession. It is important that the coach should be the one to decide when and why the team must use these tactics – in relation to the defense strategy that he has decided to adopt. In this section we will give some advice that must not be followed to the letter and that should only be applied when it can be integrated with the defense philosophy applied by the team. It is a good idea to apply offside tactics when:

- The defenders are in *numerical inferiority* with respect to the strikers. In situations of numerical inferiority it is a good idea for the defense section to move backwards to the limit of the penalty area in order to favor the possible recovery on their team mates' part; they will then very quickly move into depth towards the ball, one or two players coming out to put pressure on the player in possession and the others tightening up and trying to take up position on the passing lines.

- We are facing opponents whose players are better than we are in the air and who exploit their skill setting up plays that develop from instant *long passes* towards the strikers. We must always keep in mind that the longer the pass or the free kick the more difficult it will be for the referee to decide whether the strikers are in an irregular position or not when the ball is kicked.

- When you need to *regain possession as quickly as possible* because you are not satisfied with the ongoing result. Along with pressing, offside tactics are one of the most important means of regaining possession as quickly as possible. With a few minutes to go in a match, you might have to risk everything in order to be able to play a few more balls in the attacking phase.

HOW TO APPLY OFFSIDE TACTICS WITH SUCCESS

Using offside tactics without adequate organization means running gigantic risks. Let us therefore try to have a good look at the characteristics that will make sure using offside is not a risk, but a means at the service of the team helping them to regain possession and forcing the adversaries to attack in ways that will be more difficult for them.

- Good *pressure on the player in possession*; (if the player in possession is contrasted by one or more opponents it will be difficult for him to move forward with the ball. He can pass to a team mate breaking into space, but this second player will not find it easy to elude the offside trap).
- The defense section's ability to *move forward in a compact way, quickly and with the right timing*; (the movement into depth must be sharp, the players coming forward must be in a line and all this must be done when there is strong pressure on the player in possession).
- *Knowing your opponents* and being sure that they are not really capable of applying the right countermoves to offside tactics.
- *Do not use offside tactics in a systematic way*, but only in relation to certain tactical situations, so as to be unpredictable and not to give precise points of reference to the opponent's countermoves.

A DEFINITION OF THE ELASTIC (OR WAVE-LIKE) DEFENSE

The elastic (or wave-like) defense is when the entire defense section of the team move into depth and backwards (as required by the tactical situation) in a coordinated way during the defense phase.

WHAT IS THE ELASTIC DEFENSE FOR?

When the backs are using the elastic defense their aim is to not give depth to their opponent's play, allowing the defending team to 'shorten up' and to have numerical superiority around the ball.

THE ELASTIC: THE MOVING UP PHASE AND THE MOVING BACK PHASE

Using offside in an *active way* involves moving your defense line into depth, so forcing the attacking players to go backwards in order not to find themselves in an offside position. It is important, therefore, that, for every forward movement of the ball following on the opposition's offensive play, there must be a corresponding movement of our defense line into depth. If we are to speak of offside tactics at all, that is the necessary condition: the defense section moves up at the same time that the ball moves down towards the goal that they are defending. On the other hand, in cases where the attacking team passes the ball backwards, the defense line do not then carry out their in-depth movement to put their opponent's in an offside position but to keep themselves at the right distance from the mid fielders, who will be moving upwards at the same time to go in contrast on the player in possession, now placed further backwards than before. The elastic forward movement of the defense section is associated, therefore, with the movements of the mid fielders, and its purpose is, first of all, to keep the team as compact as possible, and, secondly, to cut out any possibility for the opposing strikers to move subsequently into depth. You must be careful however: on one hand, the forward movement may make it impossible for the strikers to attack in depth, but on the other it will favor the mid fielders' subsequent cuts as they try to break into the area. To avoid this, it is important that, at the moment the adversary has received a back pass and is ready to play the ball forwards, the two center defenders should stop and go back a couple of yards so that the attacking team cannot successfully insert their mid fielders. It is this backwards and forwards movement of the defense section that resembles the movements of a wave or of a vibrating elastic band.

94

It should also be pointed out that you can take depth out of your opponent's plays by both moving up or down. As we have shown, it stands to reason that the forward movement of the defense section will not allow the strikers to go into depth; it is relatively clear as well that the strikers will find it practically impossible to be ready for a winning cross if they are arriving behind the defending players while they in turn are moving quickly backwards.

TO SUM UP:

The defense section moves into depth:

- at the same moment as the back pass (i.e., accompanying the movement of the ball);
- until they get into a position that makes it impossible for the opposition to play the ball forward (covered ball);
- when they are applying offside in the active mode.

The defense section moves backwards:

- the moment the opponent in possession is able to play the ball forward and launch a team mate who is breaking in from behind the defense line (uncovered ball);
- whenever you want to stop the opposition from going into depth, as, for example, in a situation of numerical inferiority (the section slips backwards so as to slow down the adversary's play and to give a team mate time to get back into a position that is more useful from a tactical point of view).

APPENDIX 2

MOVING INTO THE OFFENSE PHASE OR COUNTERATTACKING

MOVING OUT OR COUNTERATTACKING

Pressing is not a collective tactic that you carry out just for the fun of it. The way in which you regain possession of the ball will greatly influence the following offense phase (sometimes called 'moving out'). By making a detailed study of the characteristics of each of his players, the coach must put them into the best conditions to take advantage of the attacking phase; but he must also define the type of pressing suitable for the counterattack. Before going on, we must take a brief look at a couple of things that are usually considered obvious. It is generally said that if we have fast attacking players it is better to let the opponents move down field (while we use low level pressing) so that our players will have space to attack in depth. Or, on the contrary, if we have a big but slow attack, it is better to carry out in-depth pressing so than we can more easily manage to cross the ball. I believe the initial management of a ball whose possession we have just regained will be vitally important for the subsequent counterattack – and not only the actual zone where we enter into possession. That initial management of the ball is what I call the *consolidation phase*, and – depending on the tactical situation on the field and the strategic choices defined by the coach – it can be developed in various different ways.

If, when we have intercepted the ball, we have to start looking for a supporting player on whom to dump it in order to begin an elaborate build up – then, of course we will find it difficult to accelerate or to go for immediate depth. When, instead, the players have been told to go at once for the vertical pass – the actions set up by the team will be quicker and so much deeper.

If you wish to develop fast and effective counterattacks you must give the following points of reference to the team:

- always give support to the player who has taken back possession (in cases where he is not able to move up with the ball);
- organize in-depth movements on the part of the attacking section (the striker nearest to the ball carries out the basic movement; his team mates' cuts will interact on these).

In order to perfect your counterattacks, the strikers' movements must be synchronous, and those movements must take place when the team mate in possession is in a favorable situation to play the assist or to filter a pass.

The coach must use the right methods to teach the team to:

- speed up as much as possible his team's positive transition;
- organize combinations in the movements of the strikers who are going into attack in depth;
- give the player who has regained possession the chance to move up with the ball or to dump on a supporting player,
- perfect the timing of collective play.

TRAINING THE POSITIVE TRANSITION – ORGANIZING THE MOVEMENTS OF THE ATTACKING SECTION

As we have already seen, we can create immediate counterattacks with both the same player who has taken back the ball or with a supporting player to whom it has been dumped. Here are some exercises which will help to define and improve the cooperation between the player regaining possession and his support:

EXERCISE 1: GIVING A SOLUTION TO THE PLAYER IN POSSESSION

On the whole field our 'sparring partners' are passing the ball around, obliging our players to simulate pressing. At the coach's whistle, our team must start pressing actively in order to regain possession. Once he has taken back the ball, the new player will have to dump it as quickly as possible on a supporting team mate.

Apart from organizing emergency solutions (dumping on a player in support), the coach will also have to train the skills of the player who has regained possession to go off with the ball at his feet. In order to do this, some theme training matches could be organized.

EXERCISE 2: PERFECTING YOUR TIMING

The players carrying out the assists or the cuts will need good timing, and this can be improved with the following exercises:
On a regular sized field the team simulates pressing by going in to attack the balls placed on the field (the coach indicating which ball they are to go for). When the signal is given, the player nearest to the ball pretends to have taken possession of it and begins the counterattack by making an pass to the strikers breaking into depth.

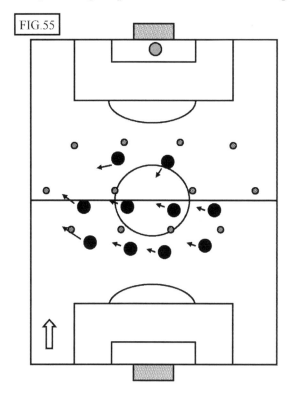

FIG.55

Using different signs, you can also tell the player taking possession whether to move up with the ball at his feet or look for a supporting player (one whistle = moving with the ball + seeking a pass into depth; two whistles = looking for support). This exercise trains the players to time their plays – assists or cuts – in simple situations (without the presence of opponents on the field).

In the second exercise there will be another team on the field as a sparring partner, whose job it is to pass the ball from one side of the field to the other. The team being trained will have to follow the movements of the ball, and, when the signal is given, regain possession, (the adversaries should not stop them in an active way). The exercise will continue as in the one previously described, with the team that takes possession looking for immediate depth. The presence of the sparring partner's defense section means that the strikers will have to connect their movements, not only with their team mates in possession – as in the last exercise – but also with the opposing defense section as in a real match. In particular the attacking players must not be too far away from the opponent's defense line (because otherwise they will run the risk of not having time to attack them from behind), and it is also important to make sure that the direction and the tempo of their play do not put them into an offside position. During the exercise we could also ask the sparring partner's defending group to simulate the movements of the defense section belonging to the team we are about to meet (e.g. offside, playing for time etc.). A possible problem that can come up after systematic repetition of this type of exercise is that our defense section could quite naturally get too used to the strikers' in-depth movements (knowing that the strikers are going to try and break into space, the defenders will automatically move backwards). As far as senior teams are concerned, we can resolve this type of problem by getting the teams from the youth sector to act as sparring partners. They will attempt to play for time of course, but that will be compensated for by the fact that they will be slower in their movements.

The third and last exercise is a theme match with one (or both) teams trying (in the right conditions) to create attacking play in the form of moving up or immediate counterattacking.

Also Available from Reedswain

Also Available from Reedswain